OF W(

What they don't teach: Handy
tips for coping

Charlotte Mweemba

ISBN: 9798357246455

DEDICATION

To Rachel and Sharon "Mama'

ACKNOWLEDGMENTS

I would like to express my profound gratitude to my wonderful friends and family for their unwavering love and support. Special thanks to my life guru Daniel, Vichaya, Mable, Ndita, Natalie, Lushomo, Suzyo, Luyando, Chuchu, Chiku, Bwalya, Thomas and Makisa, for their invaluable contribution and for making this publication possible.

CONTENTS

INTRODUCTION

Women are a special creation. The sustenance of human life depends on women.

Although similar in our biological make-up, we are endowed with diverse personalities and intellectual capabilities just as we are in our upbringing, education and life experiences. Growing up as a woman has its joys and challenges. We are taught the basics of life, usually through the socialisation process, which has a role, along with our own individuality, in determining our interpretation of our life experiences and how we react to them. There is no such thing as the school of life. Each one of us must experience our own individual life and deal with it.

This book highlights basic life lessons that are often not taught, formally or informally, but that greatly impact women, with examples of real-life experiences. The identities and names of the people referred to in this book have been changed to protect them.

CHAPTER 1
OF BEAUTY

'Something that the human race has forgotten. Beautiful is often used synonymously with hot or sexy. This is not the case. No, body fat and large breasts do not make a girl beautiful. Beauty is a pure, non-sexual thing. It comes from the right combination of personality, confidence and (of course) physical attraction'—Queen Frostine

You are beautiful just the way you are. Every woman is endowed with immense and unique beauty and strength, regardless of their circumstances and physical appearance. Society has imposed its own definition of beauty, often depicted in the media as a slim, flat tummy and a small waistline. The reality is that beauty is more than meets the eye. Beauty means different things to different people. We are all different and beautiful in our individuality.

For most women, weight loss is a touchy topic.

Many women struggle with their weight, especially as they get older. The fat just appears to unapologetically sit in all the 'wrong' places. The once upon a time perfect body starts changing, add childbearing it does not get better. The body has no problem absorbing an extra pound but has a big problem giving it up. Being over-weight, can impact your self-esteem and confidence as a woman. Too many have gone to their graves without comprehending, appreciating and utilizing the beauty that they possessed, looking down on themselves.

With changing times, the concept of the beauty of a woman has also been evolving. According to Robin Givhan from the magazine *Women of Impact* for National Geographic in his profound words says, 'the idea of beauty is always shifting. Today it is more inclusive than ever......the definition of beauty has continued to expand, making room for women of colour, obese women, women with vitiligo, bald women, women with grey hair and wrinkles. We are moving toward a culture of big tent beauty. One in which everyone is welcome. Everyone is beautiful.'

How beautiful you are is entirely up to you to decide. The concept of beauty is broad. There is no one-size-fits-all. This is depicted by the never-seen-before inclusion of some high-end fashion lines, who have adopted plus-sized categories to their clothes lines to embrace the diversity of women's beauty. We have also seen the unprecedented inclusion of models with Down's syndrome and autism being added to the model list for luxury brands such as Victoria's Secret. The diversity of beauty.

It is important to feel comfortable in your own body, at whatever point you are at. Our lack of self-esteem sometimes stems from media perceptions of beauty or insensitive remarks about parts of our bodies made by other people, which become so entrenched in our minds that they become a reality. I have a short nail bed and naturally short nails and growing up, that became a reason to be ridiculed by my older sisters, something that left me so conscious of my nails that it took me till adulthood to appreciate them. Your confidence is projected by the esteem in which you hold yourself.

Remember, your appearance affects the way you are perceived by others, which in part determines how people will relate to you. As women, our self-perception goes to the core of our self-confidence. Keeping healthy and maintaining clean, well-kempt hair, nails, clothes and sometimes even make-up all go a long way in accentuating our beauty and boosting our self-confidence. Regardless of your weight, shape, colour, means, disability, height or any other measure, there will always be fashion options available to make your beauty shine and your overall appearance stand out. We must accept ourselves just as we are.

According to Golda Poretsky, 'body acceptance means, as much as possible, approving of and loving your body, despite its imperfections, real or perceived. That means accepting that your body is fatter than some others or thinner than some others, that your eyes are a little crooked, that you have a disability that makes walking difficult, that you must deal with-but that all of that doesn't mean that you need to be ashamed of your body or try to change it. Body acceptance allows for the fact that there is a diversity of bodies in the world, and that there is no wrong way to have one'.

Therefore, forget about being too big, too small, too fat, too thin, too tall, or too short, or too. Anything. You should love and embrace yourself because you are perfect just the way you are. There is, after all, only one you.

'And the globalization of, well everything means that somewhere out there is an audience that will appreciate you in all your magnificent………….. whatever. We are all beautiful.' — Anon.

CHAPTER 2
OF CONFIDENCE, STRENGTH AND ASSERTIVENESS

'A strong woman understands that the gifts such as logic, decisiveness and strength are just as feminine as intuition and emotional connection. She values and uses all her gifts- Nancy Rathburn

Women are endowed with immense strength. We often get beaten up by life's experiences so that we lose our confidence, overlooking our potential. Sometimes, we choose to remain silent when we know deep inside that we must speak. We are so scared of saying the wrong things and being shot down, misunderstood, laughed at, or ridiculed even when we know we are right. Sometimes, it's the wrong answers that make us grow.

Years ago, I attended a meeting that erroneously proceeded without following one critical process that would have rendered the entire proceedings void. Instead of asserting myself by bringing my observation to the attention of the facilitator, nervous about being misunderstood or judged as overzealous, I whispered my observation to a male colleague that was seated next to me, who without hesitating, rose to bring the error to the attention of the facilitators. Of course, he never gave credit to me in his submission. All the credit and glory went to him. That's what you get for knowing stuff and keeping it to yourself.

Women will sometimes endure abuse just because they are afraid of what people will think or say, or what the perpetrator of the abuse might do, or whether anyone will even believe their story. A twenty-two-year-old young woman struggled with abuse from an older co-worker who made it a point to stand at the door and brush her breast with his arm every day when she arrived in the morning and when she was leaving, while faintly uttering obscenities. Afraid to express herself, she put up with it for a few days, praying it would stop. It didn't. She was losing control. After a week, she had had enough, garnered enough strength and, in an outburst, demanded that he stops it or else she would have him reported. It never happened again. It was her body, and she took her power back and put an end to it.

Confidence does and should not only stem from academic excellence, good looks, or other petty attributes. Confidence must stem from within. The world is full of millionaires who were school dropouts. Many a time, what were straight "A" students in school remain behind and the not too brilliant ones reach much higher heights because they tap into every available resource, besides academia, to leverage the opportunities that abound. Regardless of your circumstances, there is a star waiting to be activated in each one of us, ours is to find it.

Take Queen Cleopatra of Egypt, who in 48 B.C. was exiled by her brother from Egypt. One night, as Caesar, the great Roman leader, was visiting Egypt and entertaining at the Egyptian Palace, a guard entered and informed him that he'd received a gift from a Greek merchant. The gift was wrapped in a carpet and when unwrapped, there arose half-dressed Cleopatra. A relationship developed, and he was captivated by her beauty and charm. Caesar left Rome, opting to spend more time in Egypt with his lover, away from his throne. After Caesar's death, Cleopatra invited his successor Mark Anthony to meet her in the Egyptian town of Tarsus. At first sight, he was enthralled by her appearance, enchanted by her charm and the two became lovers. It is written that, "the charm of Cleopatra's presence was irresistible and there was an attraction in her person and talk, together with a peculiar force of character which pervaded her every word and action." You can read more Robert Green's *The Art of Seduction*.

Cleopatra was not given to good looks, for there were many more beautiful than her. Her strength lay in the confidence she had in herself and her limitless possibilities. Cleopatra, above all women, constantly transformed herself and used her strengths to attract attention and get what she wanted. This is why she remains the one woman that had the most profound influence on Egyptian politics to the extent that we still read about her today and movies have even been produced to depict her life.

Seek to develop and maintain your confidence. Accept your own beauty and individuality. Never talk yourself down. You don't have to conform to the standards of others — make your own. People who are confident, assertive, and expressive are more likely to be noticed, climb any ladder they desire, and get what they want.

'To be passive is to let others decide for you. To be aggressive is to decide for others. To be assertive is to decide for yourself. And to trust that there is enough, that you are enough'—Edith Eva Eger .

CHAPTER 3
OF ACRES OF DIAMONDS

'Your diamonds are not in far distant mountains
or in yonder seas; they are in your own backyard,
if you but dig for them'— Russel H. Conwell

The book, *Acres of Diamonds*, written by Russel Conwell
in 1921 is full of old wisdom, and profound lessons.
Russel tells a story about a wealthy and contented man
who owned a large farm full of orchards, grain fields
and gardens. He met an old priest who told him about
diamonds, describing them in all their splendour, value
and power. The old priest explained to the farmer how,
with diamonds, he could purchase the entire country
and place his children on thrones through the influence
of their great wealth. After listening to the story of
diamonds, the already wealthy farmer went to bed
discontented and feeling poor. Disgruntled, he sold his
farm and set out to find the diamonds, leaving his
family in the care of neighbours.

He was never able to find the diamonds that he had given up everything for. In his quest to find the diamonds, he spent all his money and lost everything. Failing to cope with his predicament, he threw himself into the sea and died. The buyer of his farm went out to the stream within the farm to give his camel a drink and as the camel put its nose down, he noticed a curious flash of light from the sands in the shallow stream. It was a black stone, revealing the colours of the rainbow. On inquiry, he discovered that it was a diamond. It is said the great Kohinoor diamond in England's crown jewels came from that mine.

The wealthy farmer left his farm to look for diamonds elsewhere, even allowing himself to die from abject poverty and depression, when he had diamonds lying right in the back of his farm and he didn't know it.

There are so many such stories and each day we make the same mistakes in our day-to-day lives. Fervently searching elsewhere for things, we already have. This story depicts the consequences of being discontent, failing to think through decisions and authenticate information, lack of gratitude for what is, where you are and what you have in your hand and failing to make use of it.

We tend to look outside of ourselves and situations for solutions and answers that lie right within our reach or even ourselves and we lose sight of our vision and our hopes and dreams in the process, just like the wealthy farmer.

Remember, there lie acres of diamonds around us. All we need to do is search and they will be found.

'When you are tempted to look elsewhere for

greener pastures, just remember someone else is probably looking at yours. And if another pasture looks greener, perhaps it is getting better care and attention. Grass is always greener...... when it watered' —Ezra Taft Benson.

CHAPTER 4
OF GOOD MANNERS (ETIQUETTE)

'Good manners will open doors that the best education cannot'—Clarence Thomas

Your conduct both in private and public speaks volumes about you. It is cardinal that you are well versed in good etiquette, particularly in public, to ensure that you exhibit culturally acceptable behaviour. This rule applies to all platforms of interaction and communication (verbal and written): face-to-face encounters, phone conversations, emails, letters, and social media. My recent book, *Etiquette Gems Revealed*, elaborates the basics of contemporary etiquette.

Well-bred or not, the good news is that these skills can be acquired, and they must be acquired as they are necessary for any social interaction. Good manners are about being graceful. We have all met people that are so outrightly uncultured. Speaking on top of their voices in a public place or while on the phone, yelling and, talking loudly with food in their mouth are all behaviours that make heads turn. The result, people will immediately form an opinion about the person and inwardly resent and distance themselves from such a person. You don't want that to be you.

There is a need to show respect for yourself and others at all levels of our lives.

Knowing how to behave around people is important. Knowing what to say and how to say it (such as contentious issues like sex, politics, religion, sexual orientation, hate speech, or gossip with people you are not well acquainted with), how to dress appropriately, all culminate to determine how you will be perceived by other people and in turn how they will relate to you.

Exuding grace and good etiquette in our day-to-day interactions with other people will always yield benefits.

'Better good manners than good looks'—
Proverb

CHAPTER 5
OF NETWORKING AND BUILDING RELATIONSHIPS

'Networking is not about just connecting people. It's about connecting people with people, people with ideas and people with opportunities'— Michele James

Networking is the formal or informal process of engaging with others with the aim of forming social or other relationships. Networking involves interacting with others. Sometimes, this can be a once-off, while other times, the interaction develops into a more solid social or business relationship.

Networking is, however, not always a random process and should sometimes be strategic. They say money is in people's pockets. Therefore, to have legal access to it, you must meet those people and ascertain areas of common interest that may present an opportunity for future business. To create an opportunity to meet certain people, you must go to the right places, dress the right way, behave the right way and say the right things in the right manner. On a first date, avoid discussing the four "no-nos," which are sex, politics, religion, and sexual orientation. These are the infallible ingredients to draw the other person's interest in you.

Exuding grace and politeness with a smile, especially on the first encounter, will never disappoint. It demonstrates pleasantness and a genuine interest in the other person on the first encounter.

Building networks is critical, even for women. Although in interacting, especially with the opposite sex, it is important to draw the necessary boundaries. Factors ranging from dress, demeanour, laugh, voice projection, body language and conversation all come into play in determining the other person's perception of you and how they will relate to you. Ensure that you engage by conversing—listen, speak and allow the other person to speak too. A skimpy skirt, revealing top and heavy jewellery at a business breakfast may not be very helpful in projecting the desired professional image, regardless of how smart you might be. Therefore, there is a need for mindfulness in ensuring that a positive image of yourself is portrayed in networking.

There is no limit to the relationships you can create with other people. Building relationships is necessary in the general scheme of things. Networks are the platforms through which millionaires are born. We must seek to seize opportunities to meet and interact with people and build relationships whenever we can. People's networks are not written on their foreheads. You will only know who they are, who they know and how they know them if you become a part of their network. You just never know when it's time to call upon that relationship and how far it can take you.

'Networking is marketing. Marketing yourself, your uniqueness, what you stand for'—Christine Comaford-Lynch.

CHAPTER 6
OF APOLOGIES

'Apologising does not always mean that you're wrong and the other person is right. It just means that you value your relationship more than your ego'—Unknown

From an early age, we are taught to apologise when we hurt others. An apology soothes the soul of the offended person. The word "sorry" brings healing to relationships that would otherwise be permanently damaged. Building relationships usually takes time and commitment, and such relationships, if constructive, must be nurtured and protected. When there is a threat to a valuable relationship, we must endeavour to mend it. If the threat is because of your wrongdoing, then it is prudent to apologise.

An apology is one of the cheapest and yet invaluable tools that exist for the sustenance of human relationships. An apology takes a fraction of a second to say but failure to render can break down relationships that have taken years to build. An apology has never killed, changed or taken anything from anyone.

When wrongdoing has been done to another, whether intentionally or unintentionally, through words, deeds, or other means, sincere and unambiguous apologies should be rendered. In chatting with a couple one day, the wife complained that each time her husband had offended her, and she expressed how she felt, his response was always, "okay fine, then I am sorry". That line, the half-hearted apology, only succeeded in aggravating their differences. An unqualified apology like, "I am so sorry. I didn't mean to hurt you" is more sincere than the former. Apologies should be genuine and unfeigned and not made just for the sake of peace and the sustenance of a relationship.

Sometimes there is a tendency to apologise and take responsibility for a partner's mistake even when they are not at fault. This is particularly common in abusive relationships. Some men are endowed with the ingenious art of turning tables against their partners, guilt-tripping them for their own wrongdoing. Take Catherine, who found her husband walking out of a motel room, hand in hand with another woman. Hysterical, she approached them, causing a scene, prompting her husband to run off to his car for safety, driving off with the other woman, leaving Catherine in tears. He arrived home later that evening, writhing with anger at the embarrassment his wife had caused him. Catherine, rather than deal with the issue of the apparent infidelity, instead profusely apologized for over-reacting and causing him embarrassment.

Catherine and her husband did not deal with the real issue at hand. By unilaterally apologising, she threw the dirt under the carpet.

We all know that dirt under the carpet does not remove itself, all it does is accumulate until one day when the carpet can no longer sustain it.

Whether we offend strangers, co-workers, employees, children, partners, family or whomsoever, humanity dictates that we should render a sincere and unqualified apology. A fraction of a second is all it takes to say sorry.

We must however, not forget ourselves and allow circumstances or other people's wrongdoing to compromise our integrity and self-worth.

'An apology is the super glue of life. It can repair just about anything'—Lynn Johnston.

CHAPTER 7
OF BOUNDARIES

'Love yourself enough to set boundaries. Your time and energy are precious. You get to choose how you use it. You teach people how to treat you by deciding what you will and won't accept'—Anna Tylor

Each day, we interact in various ways with family, friends, co-workers, business associates, the public and a whole lot of other people, albeit strangers at different levels. The degree of familiarity, distance, or proximity between you and these third parties depends entirely on your relationship with them. Your child can surely jump into bed with you, your best friend might spend a night at your house and very well enter your bedroom, while others can only come in as far as the living room, while others only end up at the office. When an 'unqualified' person enters any of our personal spaces, uninvited, we get offended. All these situations define non-verbal boundaries, personal spaces or distances we keep from different people.

Psychologists have defined these psychological distances between people in terms of the extent of their emotional boding as they communicate. Edward T. Hall categorises the interpersonal distances of human beings (relative distances between people) into four distinct zones, namely, intimate space, personal space, social space, and public space. Intimate space is the distance that allows for very personal engagement such as touching and whispering, estimated at between 1 cm and 46 cm. Personal space allows for interaction between friends and family and lies between 46 cm and 122 cm. Personal space is the region surrounding a person which they ordinarily regard as their own space and feel anxiety or anger if it is trespassed upon, like a thief entering your handbag. Social distance/space (which term now resonates with the Covid-19) is the distance maintained between individuals in a social context, such as those of different social, ethnic, cultural, occupational, religious or other groups from their own. This space is located between 1.2 m and 3.7 m, whereas public space is located between 3.7 m and 7.6 m and above, and is the space at the far end of any psychological distance that humans operate or function[i].

These boundaries are key in keeping and maintaining comfortable physical distances or boundaries between people. They are our psychological safety nets.

If a person in our intimate, personal, or even social space conducts themselves in a way that breaks certain boundaries, they can lose the privilege of being in that space, as in the case of an ex-lover. Regardless of the degree of closeness, no single individual has the carte blanch right to one's person's space.

For example, your money is yours. Your pocket is sacred. No one, whether family, partner, brother, or sister, friend or foe is entitled to your money, as a matter of course. Take the case of Cindy, who had been in and out of relationships and ran a successful business. Cindy had long been desperate for a stable relationship and then came Michael. Cindy was the higher earner and to get Michael's love and attention, she spoilt him with gifts, clothe and money. One day, while on trip out of town, Cindy began receiving notifications of large purchases from her account and whose debit card she had left home. One of those transactions was from a popular five-star hotel. Out of concern, she called Michael to explain what was going on and he admitted taking the card from her handbag, having mastered the pin and using the funds without her knowledge or permission to entertain himself and his friends. She had allowed it. Michael had broken boundaries. She had to reset the boundaries.

What is yours, in whatever form, is yours. You set the boundaries and have the power to decide what is and is not permissible. While the circumstances of breaking boundaries may vary, the moral of the story is that boundaries exist for a reason and must be preserved as such. Tolerating other people's indiscriminate violations of our personal spaces and boundaries should not be accepted.

'Boundaries protect the things that are of value to you. They keep you in alignment with what you have decided you want in life. That means the key to good boundaries is knowing what you want.'—

Adelyn Birch.

---

[i] Constable, Anne (24 July 2009). Edward T. Hall, 1914-2009: Anthropologist, personal spaces.

CHAPTER 8
OF LETTING OUT TOO MUCH

'All human beings have three lives: public, private and secret'—Gabriel Garcia Marquez

The adage that people only know what we tell them remains true to this day. You need to know what to let out, how much to let out, who to let it out to and when to let it out, if you should. We have probably all been in a place where we have said too much and prayed that the person with whom we shared the story kept it to themselves. Whether it's a first meeting, an acquaintance, a friend, a business or romantic partner, or a family member, there should always be boundaries regarding how much they can and should know.

Letting out information about the sordid things we did in the past, abusive relationships, or traumatic childhood may be necessary to divulge depending on the necessity and the person with whom it is shared. However, there is a time and place for the disclosure of certain information.

While it is important to be open, they are stages in the development of each relationship. Some relationships will earn the right to know certain information about us, but not others. Personal information must be shared on a need-to-know basis.

People do not usually like people associated with any kind of drama and will run at the slightest scent of it. A friend on a first date sat there listening to her date tell her about a ride he had given female hitchhiker on a highway and who, in the middle of their journey, asked him to put down the music. He got very offended and stopped the car 30 km from the nearest town and right in the middle of nowhere, asked her to get out of his car and left her standing ther. That was enough for her to ensure that he saw no second date.

Avoid sharing those stories before the time is right. Take it one day at a time. Keep some to yourself. There is a person, a time, and a place for full disclosure. If the person, time, and place are not ripe, keep it.

'You gotta be careful: don't say a word to nobody about nothing anytime ever'—Johnny Depp

CHAPTER 9
OF SAYING 'NO'

'No is a complete sentence. It does not require an explanation to follow. You can truly answer someone's request with a simple no'— Sharon Rainey

We often unconsciously allow ourselves to be manipulated by others owing to either, our need to be liked, not to hurt others or be judged by our failure to say no when we should.

Elizabeth, a single mum, worked 12 hours a day trying to make ends meet, providing for child and her partner. An able-bodied grown man who chose to stay home eating popcorn and watching television, giving the excuse that there were no jobs available for his skill. To her, the emotional benefits of the relationship outweighed the financial stress she had to endure to for its sustenance. Over time, he started drinking excessively and became abusive. She continued to enable his drinking habits until she reached a tipping point, abruptly ending the relationship. Elizabeth would have saved herself money and enjoyed a stress-free life, had she said "no" from the outset.

We fail to say no to being bullied, manipulated, hurt, abused, having our authority under-mined by others in so many situations, knowing that we must. Whatever the situation, you have a right to say NO.

"NO" is a two-letter word that only takes a millisecond to say.

The consequences of failing to say no, can be devastating. If you are in doubt or it makes you uncomfortable and you know it's not right, just say NO or the barest minimum, "Let me think about it", then say "no" afterwards.

Remember, 'you can be a good person with a kind heart and still say no'—Lori Deschene.

CHAPTER 10
OF PEOPLE'S OPINIONS & RUNNING YOUR OWN RACE

'If you fuel your journey with the opinions of others, you are going to run out of gas'—Steve Maraboli

When faced with a decision-making situation, our first instinct is often the right course of action. However, we are often inclined to disregard our gut instinct and seek the opinion of others.

A case in point is Sally, who took out a 20-year mortgage, at a time when interest rates were low. Governments changed and interest rates began to soar, skyrocketing to nearly double, which increased her monthly repayments, causing a huge strain on her pocket. She lived in the mortgaged property. Sally was approached by an agent regarding the sale of land in a new development area in proximity to both her workplace and children's school. The location was perfect for the construction of a new home, or alternatively, for rental property.

She had made considerable improvements to the mortgaged property, which sat in a prime location. The going price for the house would not only enable her to settle the outstanding balance but also to purchase the land in the new development area, and construct a standard house. She was in gainful employment and decided to engage the services of a realtor to facilitate the sale. A week later, there came a buyer offering to purchase the mortgaged property at a price higher than she had anticipated.

Then Sally decided to seek the opinions of others. Her sister advised her not to sell the property because she would never be able to buy an alternative house in that location and at that price. Someone else told her the property it had too much sentimental value to be sold, another said construction was too much work and only one thought it was a brilliant idea. She lost focus, changed her mind, never sold the house, didn't settle the mortgage and the interest rates continued to soar. A few years later, her work contract was not renewed, and she could no longer afford the mortgage payments. Four years later, she sold the property at the forced sale value, paid off the mortgage and could not afford to get another property in the same area as prices had gone up. Therein lies the power of seeking opinions.

It's not wrong to seek the objective opinions and counsel of others on some issues but in so doing, take care not to lose sight of your own independent judgment. Douglas Adams wrote, 'All opinions are equal. Some are a very great deal more robust, sophisticated, and well supported in logic and argument than others.'

It is not everything that requires a second or even third opinion.

I had occasion to interact with a woman that had just retired and was far from ready for retirement, having been heavily indebted. She was offered a subsequent three-year contract by her former employer, which she declined. She had 3 unemployed adult children and 2 grandchildren that were dependent on her. She was constantly financially stressed. When asked why she had declined the offer for the three-year contract, considering her circumstances, her reply was, 'People were going to laugh at me'. She had been handed an opportunity to mitigate her situation but chose to base her decision solely on other people. Her life thereafter took a downward spiral and the rest is history.

The reality is that people will always have something to say. Whether you cut your hair short or keep it long, gain or lose weight, there will always be an opinion. Situations may arise where people's potential reactions should be considered. Where necessary, endeavour to make your own objective assessment of the circumstances in arriving at a decision rather than rely on what other people will say.

The naysayers will always be with us. To always pay attention to what others say is to completely surrender your freedom to people you owe and who owe you nothing.

'How different would your life be if...............
you stopped allowing other people to dilute or poison your day with their words or opinions?

Let today be the day you stand strong in the truth of your beauty and journey through your day without attachment to the validation of others"—Steve Maraboli.

Remember how in school there were always those students who pretended not to study and yet excelled, often expressing shock at their good performance and creating the impression to everyone else that they were endowed with extraordinary intelligence.   Some of their closest peers would relax and play along, and of course not do as well as the miracle performers that seemingly did not study quite as much. There was also the crop that professed to have finished the syllabus way ahead of the class, often considering themselves smarter than the crowd, intimidating the rest.

We will meet people with these tendencies from throughout our lives in many different forms and levels. That peer that drives an assortment of luxury vehicles, lives in a fancy house, and spends lavishly on designer clothes and hand bags, that former classmate who travels across the globe posting her flawless good life on social media, that friend who runs a successful business with a 'million-dollar' annual turnover topped up with the perfect partner and children who go to the most expensive schools. Then there is you, who leads a modest life, day by day, saving, diligently watching your expenses, planning your future and that of your children., taking one day at a time. Keeping your plans and investments to yourself.

In Africa there is a saying that goes, 'don't envy your neighbours roof, you don't know what they are doing'. Many a time what seems life a flawless life is usually discreetly marred with mud. Never judge your life at any stage using the measure of other people or standards but that of your own. It's one thing to be around people who are in better place than you and who positively inspire you to reach higher heights, but it is another to be around people who make you feel inadequate because of their apparent accomplishments and status' in comparison to yours. Take one day at a time. Live your own life, run your own race., lest you drag yourself into the mud too.

'You can only run your own race. Stay in your lane. Don't look at what others are doing. Those that look back in the race usually fall off' — Oprah

CHAPTER 11
OF BEING JUDGMENTAL

"Do not judge by appearance, but judge with right judgment'-John 7:24

One common thread that runs across human beings is the tendency to judge others. We inevitably form opinions about others from the first encounter. The smile, the face, hair, the clothes, and conversations all come into play in creating our impressions of the people we meet. Sometimes, without reason, we are negative and critical of people we don't even know. We usually perceive ourselves as individuals having the most positive attributes, the best personalities, kindness, bodies, characteristics, opinions, beliefs, and even morals in judging others, often forgetting our own pitfalls. At a check-in counter at the airport, was a lady who walked in carrying a big piece of pizza and a box in her hand, chewing with her mouth open. My first impression was that she was uncouth. Inwardly I was praying that I am attended by the gentleman at the next counter, the pizza lady instead motioned to me to go to her desk. I had excess luggage, the assistance she gave me was so heart-warming. I left the counter, pinching myself for judging her so harshly. I said a big thank you and left with a big smile. Chewing pizza while she worked had no bearing on the service she provided.

The problem with being judgmental is that you are secluded and limited in your thinking about someone, so that it may prevent you from making meaningful connections and from exploring the full extent of the opportunities that may be lying in plain sight.

There's good in everyone. Keep an open mind and embrace diversity. We are all human, after all.

'Before you judge me, make sure you're perfect'—Clint Eastwood.

CHAPTER 12
OF SNITCHING

'On the road of the informer, it is always night. I cannot ever inform against anyone without feeling something die within me. I inform without pleasure, because it is necessary'— Whittaker Chambers

They say snitches get stitches. Whether they are called informers, snitchers, intelligence, whistle blowers, or whatever term they use, they have been in existence since time immemorial. Most likely, you have encountered occasions where you have intentionally or unintentionally heard, seen, smelt, or in any other manner, information about a third-party that is sensitive, confidential, mysterious, suspicious, or unusual, which if carelessly shared, would have consequences, negative or positive. It is at those times that you must decide whether to tell or not

History is full of stories of wars and other calamities

that have been averted on account of informers. History is also full of destruction that was occasioned because of informers. Relationships, jobs, and lives have been destroyed because of the disclosure of the unadulterated truth. Circumstances vary. It is prudent to bear in mind that there is a thin line between remaining silent and becoming an accomplice.

You cannot always predict how people will react to information, regardless of how well you know them. Before opening your mouth, consider first the necessity, if it is any of your business, your relationship with the intended recipient, the possible reaction and consequences of your intended actions on yourself and the person. If it's worth the risk, then go ahead.

Take Mary, who had been looking forward to getting married to the love of her life. Two weeks before her wedding, her best friend, Anne, discovered that her so-called fiancée had been dating another girl who was 8 months pregnant at the time. Mary was about to make a lifetime commitment. At the risk of ruining their friendship, Anne decided to break it down to Mary and said, "I know this might be the end of our relationship. It's a risk I am taking but I am willing to take because you must know and decide whether you want to proceed with this union or not". Well, Mary was hurt but benevolently took the information, verified it, and ended the relationship 7 days before the wedding. She is now happily married to someone else, and the rest is history. Mary was mature and level-headed enough to assess the information and make a decisive decision, which probably saved her years of drama, betrayal, and pain.

Regardless of how unpleasant the information is, if it's true, do not blame, snub, or criticize the informant.

When you do, you shut the door that might be your lifesaver, for good. People will watch you walk into ruin for fear of your reaction.

As a rule of thumb, don't believe everything you hear. People can be malicious. It is advisable to weigh and objectively assess the information and credibility of the source before you react. Remember that even the sustenance of the world's most sensitive offices depends on snitches. We need them at every level of our lives. The power of what you do with this information and how you react to it is entirely in your own hands. Be prudent.

"If there is a God, or hundreds of them, I hope they will forgive me for the harm I may have inflicted on you by telling you exactly what happened.'—Carlos Ruiz Zafon, The Midnight Palace (Niebla,#2).

CHAPTER 13
OF SOCIAL MEDIA AND PRIVACY

"Privacy is dead and social media holds the smoking gun'-Pete Cashmore

The use of social media has become rife and is constantly being used to communicate consciously or unconsciously to people, both known and unknown. Technology has cut distances off. Everyone is just a click away, through the internet and its countless platforms. A substantial part of social media platforms requires users to write, speak, use pictures, videos, and live stream, all of which can be traced back to their original source.

Unlike in-person communication, where both verbal and nonverbal cues are present, social media has no tone, making it easy to be misunderstood, necessitating caution in the content shared online. The introduction of emoji, for instance, is an attempt to create a new tone in communication on social media.

For instance, a statement made in jest may be taken seriously if not supported by a smiling emoji to soften the tone. However, the intended mellowing effect of the emojis and other facilities is not absolute.

If unregulated by etiquette and discipline, communication on social media can easily be misunderstood and even destructive to the author and other users. Everything loaded on the internet is permanent. Once you click the "send" button, it is too late. No amount of damage control can completely undo the potential damage that can result from the careless use of the internet and social media.

When putting too much information about oneself out there, caution is advised. Publications on the internet are effectively global publications. Lives have been destroyed and even lost from the reckless and unregulated use of social media over content innocently and intentionally posted on the internet without thinking or anticipating the consequences of these actions. Even soaring businesses have plummeted over careless social media publications.

The trend by several people to publicly advertise their lives on social media poses many risks to them. You have no idea who is watching, what they are thinking or feeling. A documentary on a crime channel documented the story of a woman about to get married who took to social media to share the sequence of events from her engagement counting down to her wedding. Unknown to her, her fiancé's ex-girlfriend was watching her account the entire time, started stalking her, and eventually shot her dead. The consequences of living an open life.

It is important to maintain reasonable levels of privacy and personal boundaries in the use of social media. People only know what we tell them. Private information must be shared on a need-to-know basis. The number of "likes" a posting gets is not in any way reflective of people's true feelings for you. Besides, the bulk of the time, those that view these posts don't even know you and they don't even care.

The internet has made conducting due diligence on individuals so much easier. Just google a name and all their data will be out there, including pictures. Remember, there is no opportunity to defend yourself from the impression you create of yourself on social media. So be careful what you put out there.

There is also the other category of people that are in the habit of commenting about everyone and everything on social media, even when it is outrightly none of their business, sometimes in total disregard of the feelings of others. Scathing attacks on the character and reputation of others must be avoided. Fair comment on what is necessary and constructive is the acceptable norm.

Etiquette dictates that we have a social and personal responsibility to use social media in a fair, responsible, and constructive manner, bearing in mind the potential ramifications of its abuse.

'Social media is one of the most potent tools of change in the hands of citizens. May we use it responsibly to shape the world we live in.'— Sadhguru.

CHAPTER 14
OF ADVENTURE AND RISKS

'Life is a great big canvas, throw all the paint you can on it'—Danny Kaye

Have you ever done something so out of your comfort zone that it felt thrilling? That is an adventure—exciting or daring, a moment of stepping out of your comfort zone. The comfort zone lets life pass you by. Life is a journey to be enjoyed. What is considered adventurous is subjective. Bungee jumping, hot air ballooning, and sky diving may seem like adventures to some. It is our privilege to live life, regardless of the circumstances. Marchus Purvis said, "Adventure may hurt you, but monotony will kill you."

We take risks every single day. Jumping into that car, crossing that road, getting on that flight, falling in love, marrying that partner, taking out that mortgage, that career choice, these and many more are all daily risks we face. We must take risks because they are part and parcel of life. We must do life. Without taking risks, we risk living a dull and meaningless life.

Rachel Awolchn elaborately said, "If we were meant to stay in one place, we would have roots instead of feet."

Life is fleeting, and we owe it to ourselves to make it worth our while. No one else will.

'Living with fear stops us from taking risks and if you don't go out on the branch, you're never going to get the best fruit'—Sarah Parish

CHAPTER 15
OF RELIGION

'A person does not have to be behind bars to be a prisoner. People can be prisoners of their own concepts and ideas. They can be slaves to their own selves.'-Maharaji—Prem Rawat, The Shift Network

Religious fanaticism is the obsessive and subjective enthusiasm relating to a particular religion or religious group, with all due respect, often common among certain Christian religious groups. This issue affects many women, especially the vulnerable ones. While scripture is open and available for all to read, there are different interpretations and doctrines of the same scripture by different people. Caution must be exercised in getting too deeply entrenched in religious beliefs and practices that defy ordinary reason and logic.

In some cases, people have exposed their entire

personal lives, resorting to the extent of seeking advice from religious leaders on issues that are way beyond their scope and competence. Religious indoctrination and fanaticism can be destructive and can lead to broken relationships, families, and loss of finances.

While the freedom of religion is often a guaranteed right, we must use reason and intellect in determining what to believe and what not to.

'The mind is its own place, and in itself can make heaven of hell, or hell of heaven'—John Milton, Paradise Lost

CHAPTER 16
OF AGING

'Aging is a matter of feeling, not of years'—
George William Curtis

Aging gives no warning, it just sneaks in gradually and before we know it, we look different, behave differently, our needs, wants, dress style, habits, priorities, goals and energies evolve as we get older. Those few strands of silver and grey hair that you could count eventually turn into countless strands.

People have different perceptions of aging. Others embrace it, while others repulse it. Regardless, it is an honour and privilege to be alive as many others unwillingly left this life and would have done anything, if it was within their power, to be in your shoes today. Enjoy today in all its majesty.

One of the most profound words said by a dear male friend years ago, in apparent reference to my weight gain in my mid-thirties, was, "You lose your charm at 35; after that you have to make a deliberate effort to look good and young." I didn't initially take those words seriously, but now, running well into my forties, those words couldn't be truer. We must embrace our beauty at all stages of our lives, in whatever form or shape, and take care of both our physical and mental health. Stay clean, exercise, dress nicely, wear that make-up and jewellery, look and smell good and gracefully embrace and enjoy the aging experience.

Never apologise for growing older but embrace it with grace and gratitude. They say life begins at 40. It is not too late to undo some of those wrongs. End that abusive relationship, fall in love, visit that place you've always wanted to see, go bungee jumping, tick off your bucket list. Do life!

'If life really begins on your 40th birthday, it's because that's when women finally get it.......
The guts to take back their lives'—Laura Randolph

CHAPTER 17
OF LEARNING HOW TO FISH &
FINANCIAL EMANCIPATION

'They say, 'Give a man a fish, and he'll eat for a day. Teach a man to fish and he'll eat for a lifetime.' What they don't say is, 'And it would be nice if you gave him a fishing rod'. That's the part of the analogy that's missing'-Trevor Noah, Born a Crime Stories from a South African Childhood

Many people, women inclusive, depend on other people for their sustenance, be it parents, siblings, other family members and partners. Growing into adulthood is inevitable. Circumstances change, people move, their means and priorities change, and people die, hence the necessity to strive for individual independence. There is nothing as frustrating and as degrading as living at the mercy of others.

Women, although not bestowed with physical strength, are vested with enormous and limitless potential, which unfortunately, many leave this earth without fully exploring. History is filled with great women who reached unimagined heights. Melitta Bentz, a German housewife invented the coffee filter system, Marie Van Brittain Brown, a Black woman invented the early version of the home security system. Dr. Patricia Bath was the first female African American doctor to receive a medical patent for her invention of a laser cataract treatment device called a Laser Phaco Probe in 1986. Alice Parker made the central furnace heating system using natural gas to keep homes warm, while Nancy Johnson invented the ice cream maker, and the list is endless.[ii]

Financial emancipation has long ceased to be the responsibility of husbands and governments. It is a personal responsibility. Depending on a partner, parents, friends, or others is completely unsustainable. There will always be a risk that that tap will dry and be withdrawn as circumstances change. You must take charge of your own destiny.

As a woman, your focus should be to learn how to fish—how to earn your own money and live a sustainable life, within your means and on your terms. If the extra support is there, good for you, but always make it a point to have the capacity to stand on your own regardless of the circumstances. Empowerment is the only real power a woman can ever possess. Everything else is vanity.

No matter your circumstances, you can do something, anything, to earn an honest living. If the homeless can survive day by day, so can anyone. Quit engaging in self-pity, blaming your upbringing, parents, spouses, parents, ex-partners, and everyone else for your predicament. Take your share of responsibility and be bald enough to move on. Remove those "I can't" barriers. Quit looking down on certain jobs when you know you have nothing. There's always a place to start from, So, get off that bed and that butt and do whatever it takes to earn a living.

I heard a story about a university civil engineering graduate that worked for a family as a nanny, full-time, after her graduation. She was so committed to her work that she formed a great bond with the children under her care, applying herself to the fullest. After working for a few months, there was an opening at a business owned by a friend of the family she worked for, and she got the job, instantly transforming her life. Had she opted to engage in self-pity or consider herself "too big" for the nanny role, she may never have had that opportunity. Sometimes we need to be out there with open hearts and minds and find the opportunities we seek. No one will guess you exist until they know you exist.

Humble beginnings are where most self-made millionaires started. If we just open our eyes, there's always an opportunity lurking out there. Yours is to find it.

'Millions wish for financial freedom, but only those that make it a priority have millions'— Oscar Auliq-Ice.

[ii] source www.biography.com

CHAPTER 18
OF MAD MONEY

'A part of all I earn is mine to keep. Say it in the morning when you first arise. Say it at noon. Say it at night, Say it each hour of every day. Say it to yourself until the words stand out like letters of fire across the sky'—George Clasons', The Richest Man in Babylon

A couple of years ago, I watched a movie called Mad Money, featuring Queen Latifah and Katie Holmes, a crime comedy about three women, all bank employees, struggling with different personal and financial issues. They soon come up with a scheme to steal worn-out dollar bills slated for destruction by the bank. They successfully carry out the robbery the first time and decide to continue with the theft, living large until they get caught. Just when they thought everything was lost, one of them revealed that while all of this was going on, she was stashing large amounts of cash in a secret location. There was still money to go round; it wasn't the end of the world.

Every woman needs to keep some money for emergencies. I am not saying, steal, but the movie brings to the fore the risk of being short-sighted and the necessity of preparing for the future and any eventuality.

We have heard or read about the need to save 10% of all our earnings. Financial literacy is something that is often taken for granted. Because there are many literate people who are financially illiterate. While in high school, my friend Natalie made it a point to deposit her weekly savings in her then, post office savings account each Friday after school, while we stood there and waited for her, with no idea what was going on. To this day, she preaches the need to set aside funds for retirement, unanticipated opportunities and unforeseen emergencies, and children's school fees as a pressure cushion.

Like it or not, as we age, our energy levels substantially diminish, and one day we will no longer be able to work as much or as hard as we did when we were younger. Even before the onset of old age, unforeseen events may occur in which we are incapacitated by health or any other event, and thus not able to earn an income. We must therefore individually inculcate the importance of saving money in our minds, in whatever form or manner, as those are the funds that truly remain ours, while we spend the rest. We live in an information era.

All the information on financial literacy is there on the internet, just a click away. Lessons on budgeting, prioritizing needs, how to earn and spend, and the purchase of luxury assets are all on the internet.

Circumstances vary from person to person, and there is no one size fits all in this quest for financial literacy. You must choose what works for your own individual circumstances.

.

Aging, unexpected illness or disability are all possibilities that must be prepared for. Earning and saving should go hand in hand. Love yourself enough to keep some for you.

'Do not save what is left after saving but spend what is left over after saving'—Warren Buffet.

CHAPTER 19
OF DATING

'Dating is really hard because everyone puts up a front. It's really difficult to see who is who, so it is important to be yourself.'—Brooke Burke

Dating in whatever form is primarily the process of getting to know the other person and gauging their suitability for whatever objective, relationship, marriage, or whatever endgame. There are no hard and fast dating rules. The usual basic rules: be yourself, say what you mean, say no when you are not sure, uncomfortable, or it just doesn't feel right, will always stand the test of time.

Women are generally naturally inclined to fall in love. We normally use cues to determine the depth of a potential partner's level of interest in us. It is also possible to misunderstand the message being communicated and to one-sidedly develop deep emotions for a person that doesn't quite feel the same way. To avoid this, we must endeavour to encourage open and honest communication from the outset while remaining open-minded. Keep your heart in your chest until you are sure it's safe to share it. There doesn't have to be a second date. A friend went on a first date with a guy who started video-calling her incessantly at odd hours to check-up on who she was with. She put up with him for two days and knew it was time to run.

Every person is different. Different people look for different things in potential partners, whether it's adventure, friendship, company, or marriage. They say you teach a man how to treat you. The way you start the relationship, the ground rules you set up from the outset, will govern the relationship until the end. Once these rules are set, it is very difficult to change them without misunderstanding. How does a woman who has, from day 1, taken care of all the needs of her partner, physical, emotional, and financial, suddenly get fed up and expect him to start taking care of himself or the household without facing resistance? Know what you want from a relationship and don't make compromises.

It is always better to choose a partner with a plan for their own life, especially as it relates to finances. Neither man nor woman can live on love alone. Energy is real. A hopeless partner, regardless of their good looks, will inevitably put holes in your pocket, a tragedy which might be irreversible in the long run. Take heed to your voice of reason and intuition. Use your brain and not just your heart. We have heard of men and women whose lives were greatly positively transformed and those that collapsed on account of their choice of partners.

Giving excuses for men's shortfalls is among a

woman's greatest weaknesses, even when things are obvious. Some women would be willing to give up even the sincerest of friends who dare pass the barest criticism of their partners, only to discover too late that their friend's concerns were sincere and valid.

Sometimes, we are so blinded that we don't get round to carrying out proper due diligence to ascertain who this prospective partner is. We see what we want to see. Some men are so charming that they will tell you what you want to hear. These days, even social media may provide some insight into who this prospective partner may be. That touching story about how mean or unreasonable his ex was should be taken with a pinch of salt, because many a person will tell you what they want you to know. There are two sides to every story.

Sometimes, you will find yourself believing you are better than the other woman and strive to be everything he told you she wasn't because of what you have been told.

It's so much easier to be yourself. Allow him to love or leave you exactly as you are in your uniqueness.

While dating, never lose your sense of power, especially as it alludes to the future. I have heard several women in relationships say, 'I don't know what he is thinking, I don't want to look desperate.' While it is true that overzealousness can push a potential partner away, dating is about levelling the playing field and being able to openly communicate one another's expectations of the relationship rather than leaving things to speculation. This is your life. You are a major stakeholder in the relationship and have a right to know which direction you are heading. To leave the fate of your relationship to the wind, and worse still, to another person, is to commit injustice to yourself.

Once you and your partner are on the same page, have agreed on the ground rules and have set the necessary boundaries, the relationship will flow. Speak honestly and openly; resolve differences before sunset.

Quit the silent treatment. Unresolved differences mount up like dust under the carpet and have the potential to explode and ruin the relationship in the long run. Be realistic. Don't give excuses. Use all your cues to read and understand your partner and objectively determine whether, given his apparent flaws, you can accept his continuing with the relationship, bearing in mind that you and only you will bear the consequences of any peculiarities you opt to overlook. If the relationship changes negatively and takes a form that was not intended, it's okay to walk away.

In the words of Oprah Winfrey, 'when someone shows you who they are believe them'.

CHAPTER 20
OF MARRIAGE

'The truth of the matter is that when you say 'I do', it's too late'—Anon

After hearing the story of Cinderella, it is every little girl's dream to one day wear that wedding dress, marry a prince, and live happily ever after. It is only when we grow older that we realise that Cinderella is only in fairy tales. Marriage is a beautiful thing, especially when you wind up with the right partner, but it also requires a lot of effort and compromise to sustain it.

Some rush into marriage without fully comprehending its full implications. Marriage is serious business. The choice of partner plays a fundamental role in determining which direction your entire life will go. It's a gamble. There are no guarantees. Sometimes we marry the marital status "he is single" rather than focus on our compatibility and the substance of the person we intend to commit our lives to, only to discover, after the fact, that it was a grave mistake.

Marriage is the start of a new and shared life with someone you may or may not know well, and whose union will inevitably have an impact on your future. From this union often comes children, born of both parties, who also have their own consequences for the marriage, such as added expenses and divided attention.

Sometimes, material changes in circumstances between the parties might happen. At the outset of the marriage, disability, unanticipated job loss, change in finances, discovery of a material fact that was undisclosed prior to the marriage, an intolerant partner discovered post-marriage, unreasonable in-laws, and family interference, are all examples of events that may not have been anticipated at the outset of the marriage, and which require patience and objectivity in resolving.

What makes a marriage has more to do with the relationship between the parties; how they relate to each other and react to differences between them when they occur. A sincere apology remains, by far, the greatest healer. And so is forgiveness, as is resolving to get past misunderstandings as they occur and to move on. Ranting on about things in the past has the tendency to open wounds and can be retrogressive. Respect and love are among the core foundations for a blissful marriage.

As a rule of thumb, do not allow your partner or yourself to completely alienate you from your sincere friends and family, unless it is necessary. Those are usually the third eyes that can see beyond your horizons and will usually have your best interests at heart. Never forget your individuality. Growing up, empowering yourself for death, divorce, and changes in circumstances are all risks inherent in marriage and the inevitable realities of life.

Be respectful of your partner and his privacy. Checking partners' phones, for example, has brought more harm to marriages than any other invention in world history. If you find out he's been cheating, take a deep breath, confide in someone, if you can. It is better to deal with your partner when resolving issues of infidelity and not the "other woman. Confronting the other woman might make you lose respect, look desperate, give the other person undeserving power, and, in a sense, validate the relationship. Hence, the line "even the wife knows about me" might become commonplace if the relationship doesn't end or you don't leave him. Relationships only end when both parties or one of them decides to end it, and no manner of confrontation or drama can guarantee that.

It is important for couples to embrace synergy as it promotes a healthy marriage and aids couples in combining their creative strengths and energies to achieve unimaginable success. The converse is also true. Take Steve, who married young to a very competitive woman and had a tumultuous marriage that ended in a bitter divorce. During his marriage, Steve struggled with finances and almost every area of his life, often being taunted by his wife, who constantly called him a loser. After his divorce, Steve eventually met Pamela, and the two got married. The two had mutual respect and common interests and complemented each other in many ways. Steve and Pamela harnessed their energies and worked closely together, completely transforming their lives. Together, they established a flourishing real estate business. Steve transformed from that struggling, beaten-down man with low self-esteem to an established, confident, and highly respected realtor.

It is usually the woman that sets the temple for her marriage. Respect yourself and your spouse; do not publicly mock or embarrass him. Encourage him, stand by his side, ensure he is clean and kempt, believe in him, forgive and forget, endeavour to resolve your own problems without resorting to third parties, engage, have fun. As a woman, take care of your home and yourself; look good; keep the flame burning; be open-minded; be adventurous; and always be respectful. Be cautious about who you allow into your home and ensure clear boundaries are maintained while they are there. Go out, do things together, create memories and keep the flame burning. This may sound theoretical, especially when he has caused you immense pain, but try anyway. The man must also do his part. Bear in mind that this is a book on women.

When a woman quits trying, the marriage is over.

'A good marriage isn't something you find, it's something you make and you have to keep on making it'—Gary Thomas.

CHAPTER 21
OF THE PAST, FORGIVENESS, LETTING GO AND MOVING ON

'You just do it. You force yourself to get up. You force yourself to put one foot before the other. And God damn it, you refuse to let it get to you. You fight. You cry. You curse. Then you go about your business of living. That's how I've done it. There's no other way'—Elizabeth Taylor

Life happens and sometimes you go through experiences that you later regret, often wishing if only you could turn back the hands of time, you would have made better choices and perhaps more objective decisions. The unfortunate reality is that life offers no such luck. The only route available is to forgive the past and get on with your life, from whichever place you are.

Harbouring negativity and bitterness are often because of failing to let go of the past and is usually reflected in one's attitude, which can adversely affect other relationships. Many of us have come across people, family, co-workers, friends, and foes that are so bitter to the point that they want the whole world to feel their pain. Unfortunately, that pain and anger are known only to the one harbouring them, and what is perceived by others is the negativity. People generally detest negative people.

Whether it is that traumatic childhood, an abusive relationship, or whatever negative experience you have endured, whether it is your fault or not, you must deal with it.

Take Susan, a highly qualified chief executive in a thriving organization who was in the habit of picking on at least one vulnerable subordinate at every point. She would antagonise them to the point of making them cry. On a work trip one day, after drinking a few glasses of wine, Susan, with a lot of emotion, began to tell a story of her upbringing. It turns out that she was an only child aged 5 when her mother died. Her father remarried a woman with three older children from a previous relationship. As her father's only child, she was constantly taunted by the older children, and neither her father nor stepmother tried to protect her. For years, she endured the incessant bullying with no one to run to. Susan was academically gifted and, regardless of her circumstances, had excelled in school and, eventually, university abroad on a scholarship. Through her story, the seemingly aggressive woman suddenly became vulnerable, and the pain she had endured was evident in her teary eyes. Susan had not dealt with the trauma of her childhood, and this was affecting her role as Chief Executive. Within two years, the staff had enough and revolted. The organisation's performance declined, and her contract of employment was eventually terminated.

Susan was not a bad person. Her problem lay in her failure to deal with and let go of her past, picking on people she perceived as vulnerable and making them feel her pain by taunting them as she had been taunted. Her failure to deal with her past made her counterproductive and had the potential to jeopardise her future regardless of the educational level she had attained.

People are not always aware that they have a problem. Sometimes, there may be a need for expert psychological intervention, but other times, we can strive on our own to make personal decisions and feed our minds with more positive thoughts to let go of the past.

We all make mistakes. At some point or another, we have all made bad choices that we later regret. The thoughts, 'I should have consulted, I should have taken more time to reflect, I should have known, I should have seen the signs, I should have walked away, I should have listened, I should have known, I wish I didn't have to go through all this, I wish things would have been different, I wish I hadn't done it', have come with regret. Both "I should have" and "I wish" in this context are all bygones. While the effects of these experiences can sometimes be mitigated or reversed, sometimes the damage or consequences are irreversible. What is done is done. The clock does not stop ticking and, therefore, life must go on.

Many of us are often quick to forgive others when offended but have difficulty forgiving ourselves when we make mistakes. I make it a habit to take some time off each day to reflect on the events of the day, forgiving the day in acknowledging the victories and shortcomings and resolving to do things differently going forward. Even when I make the same mistake, I run through the same process. Thereafter, quit cursing yourself for that mistake, as what is done is done. This process will not happen over-night.

Dwelling on past mistakes can take us back and inhibit our progression and ability to focus on the "now", which is the only thing we have. We need to make a conscious and deliberate effort to forgive ourselves and let go of our mistakes. It is only the lessons we draw from our mistakes that can serve us, not breathing life into past mistakes.

When a relationship of any kind becomes toxic or no longer serves its intended purpose, it's okay to let go and move on. It is only when you let go, that other opportunities open. Life will always give you second chances. Some people are not meant to move with you forever.

'You can rise from anything. You can completely recreate yourself. Nothing is permanent. You're not stuck. You have choices. You can think new thoughts. You can learn something new. You can create new habits. All that matters is that you decide today and never look back'(avertu.com).

ABOUT THE AUTHOR

Charlotte Mweemba is a Zambian-based lawyer and author with a deep love for writing and a passion for non-fiction, delving on issues of real life. *Of Women* is her second book, after her maiden publication, *Etiquette Gems Revealed*.

Cover illustration: Abstract Canvas Print Rain Modern Wall Art Painting Girl Umbrella with Red Dress Walking in Street Figure Artwork. Seekland Art.

Printed in Great Britain
by Amazon

10315050R00047